Simply Being

Roula-Maria Dib

With an introduction by Omar Sabbagh

CHIRON PUBLICATIONS • ASHEVILLE, NORTH CAROLINA

www.ChironPublications.com

Interior and cover design by Danijela Mijailovic
Printed primarily in the United States of America.

ISBN 978-1-63051-925-4 paperback
ISBN 978-1-63051-926-1 hardcover
ISBN 978-1-63051-927-8 electronic
ISBN 978-1-63051-928-5 limited edition paperback

The author would like to thank the editors of the following journals and platforms where these poems were previously published:
The Journal of Jungian Scholarly Studies, "Number 1"
Archive for Research in Archetypal Symbolism, "Starry Night, A Theogony" (as "Starry Night"), "Window of Life," "Aurora"
Indelible, "Lunar Rhapsody," "Coquelicots"
The Ekphrastic Review "When Aštart Sings," "Shoe and Tell," "Drawers, Slips and Slits," and "Nigredo" (in an article entitled "Frozen Time at London's National Gallery")
Poethead, "Ludus," "Lavenders," "Iconic Existence"
Poetry Salzburg Review, "The Prodigal Daughter"
Annahar English, "The White-in-the Waiting"
Ludus and other poems by Roula-Maria Dib were first published on the Poethead site on May 14, 2020 at https://poethead.wordpress.com/2020/05/14/ludus-and-other-poems-by-roula-maria-dib/ with thanks to editor Chris Murray.

Library of Congress Cataloging-in-Publication Data

Names: Dib, Roula-Maria, author.
Title: Simply being / Roula-Maria Dib ; with an introduction by Omar Sabbagh.
Description: Asheville, North Carolina : Chiron Publications, [2021] | Summary:
  "Simply Being is a celebration of the various facets of life, its blessings,
  beauties, and challenges. Exploring the richness of our manifold existence
  seen through the many different lenses beyond the quotidian and the
  mundane, Roula-Maria Dib looks at the multifariousness of reality and
  nuances of the self with its different roles and experiences, peeking into the
  parallel worlds of myth, and art, whichinfuse our everyday life. The poems
  in this collection are a compilation of verses on memories, aspirations,
  ekphrasis, and the different forms of love that shape us into who we are"--
  Provided by publisher.
Identifiers: LCCN 2021010163 (print) | LCCN 2021010164 (ebook) | ISBN
  9781630519261 (hardcover) | ISBN 9781630519254 (paperback) | ISBN
  9781630519278 (ebook)
Subjects: LCGFT: Poetry.
Classification: LCC PS3604.I187 S56 2021 (print) | LCC PS3604.I187 (ebook)
  | DDC 811/.6--dc23
LC record available at https://lccn.loc.gov/2021010163
LC ebook record available at https://lccn.loc.gov/2021010164

Acknowledgments

Many thanks to the editors of the journals in which many of my poems here have appeared: *The Ekphrastic Review, Poethead, The Journal of Jungian Scholarly Studies, Poetry Salzburg Review, Indelible, and ARAS.*

Huge acknowledgments, with love and thanks, are due to Omar Sabbagh and Leslie Gardner.

A special tribute to Julie and Julia, voice and verse.

About the Author

Roula-Maria Dib (PhD, Leeds) is a creative writer and literary scholar. Currently, she is a professor of English at the American University in Dubai, and editor-in-chief of *Indelible*, the university's literary journal. Her poems, essays, and articles have appeared in several journals. Her new book, *Jungian Metaphor in Modernist Literature* was published in March 2020. She is a member of the *International Association for Jungian Studies, the Jungian Society for Scholarly Studies*, and the *British Association for Modernist Studies*. The themes that pervade her work usually revolve around different aspects of human nature, ekphrasis, surrealism, and mythology.

*For Johnny and Rafaella, the rhythm behind
every verse and heartbeat, and my parents,
the reason behind my simply being.*

and

*In loving memory of my grandparents, still very
much alive through us and through the blessing
of all the love and inspiration they had given us.*

"Being is seeing in the human dimension." — Stephen R. Covey

Contents

Being About Itself

Introduction
to Roula-Maria Dib's
Simply Being

By Omar Sabbagh

Roula-Maria Dib's *Simply Being* is a poetry collection which in many ways is far from simple. Comprised of four sections, the poetry in its viscera is very much like the visceral, layered and composite. Even as a wonderful phrasemaker, Dib's collection though is more than dexterous style working through personal concerns which are both, personal at times, and more to do with her intellectual itinerary at others. That said, perhaps the one overarching manner in which this book of sparkling, intelligent and moving poems is more than just a collation of individual bits of flair and inspiration, or moments of insight, is by the way in which the personal and the intellectual marry, at times seamlessly, as though to indicate to the reader if he or she were not aware already that a sensibility such as this, inspired in many ways by Jungian psychology, strives always to express the way the individual and the universal are indeed, or might be seen to be one and the same thing.

To highlight only a few telltale phrases, titular or not, *Simply Being* is a book of verse that often names as well as illuminates a kind of "oceanic experience" which is part of "The Maze of Consciousness", or, if you prefer a kind of "Iconic Existence." There is a theme in this collection, running through it with evident urgency, which is about and about the way in which creation and creativity can be caught in the very processes of their simply being. In short, the literary artist behind these poems often, whether consciously or not (which, I suppose, must be part of the point), alights on and lights-up the artistry of being itself. Being may well be, almost by definition, the simplest thing – primarily because it is the one "thing" whose verifiable "thinghood" is unnameable and ineffable. We cannot show the being of Being, simply because we're inside it already. And yet, simply put, it seems at times in this book of verse that Dib's focal efforts strive at least to find a way back from the ontic to the ontological, as much as they involve themselves in an attempted return to the individual from the individual's dabbling with the archetypal.

In the first partition of the book, epkphrasis is used most of all, with Dib penning poetry after various choice paintings. By way of a clue-like shortcut into some of the ways in which her poetry seems indeed like the fruits and artefacts of an "iconic existence," whereby inside and outside, individual moments within poems and the poems themselves as a whole, marry in both directions, phrases like the following seem to do good work as synecdoches for the poems in which they dwell as much as for the unitive work of the book as a whole. In "Number 1," the first poem of the collection, whose title is both generic and we must assume specific to an individual act of attendance and attention to an individual painting on curated display, there are, as throughout Dib's stylistic gambits in this collection, fine examples of phrasemaking that are more redolent than mere dexterity. We read, for example, of how "Creation" is "a crowded issue," as its processes, whose disclosing and unveiling seem to be the purpose of Dib's enlivening ekphrastic poems, are seen as a "fruit-bearing fracas." This opening poem sets the tone for *Simply Being* by ending on the note of "the nothing behind the something." Close-by in "Coquelicots" the "fathomless womb" of the earth's deep (another persistent image of the roots and rooting-out of the creative process) is where and "when the blood blazes with birth." Choosing to cite such small felicitous instances might be seen to be, thus, my own iconic or metonymic indication of the overriding theme(s) and manner of the verse collected in this book. Indeed, the listing of present participles, a kind of rhetorical litany, is a syntactic tic of Dib's, but I do think that these small lists of doing and being, along with other insistent effects of alliteration and consonance, are more than merely a stylistic facet. Whether intentionally, or not, these close to semiotic effects, which are musical ways back to the body, before the logoi of denotative representation, seem again to be highly apposite for Dib's primary concerns, because they are forms of willed, chosen embodiment. And all this, might I say, without losing her grip on the quality, balance and vigor of the onrushing poems themselves.

The mythoi and overtly-named archetypal concerns, which run from "Heraclitus" to "Adonis" and "Astarte," among many others, are also places of individual biographical engagement, much as some of the more intimate poems, such as those for a grandmother or daughter seem to expose something more than immediate gestures of sincere sentiment. Self and other as much as being and nothing are not only involved in processes of generation and then regeneration, as might be simply expected from an engagement with illuminating the processes of creation or creativity, but are also often, we find out in some surprising ways, mirror images of each other, or like the two Janus-faced sides of the same coin.

"Hold my Hand," a poem after and for her own daughter, speaks of how: "I cherish the petal-softness of your fingers, / which I say bloom chubbily with time," and then, further down, closer to the poem's closing note of togetherness and mapping, then speaks of how she wonders: "for how much longer do I get to clasp it like this, / before your grip loosens in pursuit of adventure?" The blooming and the passing away, or loosening, is quite aptly clinched by the notion of pursuit and adventure. Indeed, these concepts are some of Dib's foregone and ongoing intellectual interests as a Jungian modernist, and indicate as throughout this book that the creative process, playful or serious, for others or the poet herself here, is one of growth and development; of individuation.

The Nietzschean sense of "creative destruction," which was a way for that creative philosopher to indicate the artistry of the truth of the matter as he saw it (both out there and in here) might be one way to summarize the thrust and purpose of *Simply Being*. It is a book about arising, aurorally, from the womb of the earth which takes us into its depths again – only to return. Being, if you like, about itself.

i

Number 1
On Jackson Pollock's Painting, *Number 1*

Where order is a fist, clenched around a string of fog,
chaos is the stormy sky--
dropping, like a stork,
paintbrush and chisel into the arms of
Michelangelo.
In the Sistine Chapel and the David-within-the-stone,
Creation is a crowded issue, a misty matter
where legions of feelings,
hordes of thought,
mobs of fantasies,
and layers of worlds
collude and copulate within the confused mass.
Huddling, cuddling, clouding,
Like couples of cotton candy puffs, they kiss—
dissolving into drizzly dyes,
dripping and splashing, sputtering and splattering
the shocked canvas whiteness, now blushing with
color.
From Prometheus to Pollock, chaos, the fruit-
bearing fracas, self-generating edifice,
Is a fertile exasperation,
the clamor behind the calm,
and the nothing behind the something.
It is everything.

Starry Night, a Theogony

Neurons glower on the velvety darkness of the
celestial carpet,
Sending pulses of Re, rays of light--from light,
along the axon of her longest dendrite
A stretched sciatica, Geb's root, Thoth's delight.

Meanwhile, Cassiopeia, on her heavenly throne,
Pays tribute to the dreams of days past
Granting, fusing, scattering the bulbs of thought
And no-thought, through the collective window
Of the mortal race.

Nüt stretches out her limbs, wide and tight,
Also embossing the velvety skin with diamonds.
Lapiz Lazuli softens up its shell and melts profusely,
joining in the
Gem-fest of her body.

Nüt, Nacht, Night, and Nuit,
A molten Lapiz Lazuli A café-trottoire,
A set of rolling hills,
A house with a yellow-thatched roof,
All awaken, with delight
To be tattooed on a canvas of one starry night.

Coquelicots

On Claude Monet's painting, *Poppy Fields Near Argenteuil*

Deep from within the Earth's fathomless womb,
when blood blazes with birth,
it is a blare, a bling of beauty among the sleeping
modest.
An annunciation of an *anastasis* kisses the terra
firma with the rising poppy,
whose heart of fire hides a path, a coal-black cross-
road of mystery
Well-obscured, within the flaunty scaffold,
on a red carpet by the shores of Byblos, yet in the
fields of Argenteuil.

Adonis, *puer*, a passionate call for love and life
Stands proud and eternal from the *puella*'s bosom.
With eyes of the sun, and of the night, is a rising
star--
Astarte's breath, an announcement of sunrise,
Blows over the crimson mane.
Specks of ruby awaken, scattering along the tips of
the jaded wool,
Among the humble nobility of the yellow, violet,
and indigo buds,
Swaying their heads to the crooning tunes of the

morning winds.
In the strength of the voice, the blaze of the mane,
and the dilating veins of the singing sanguine
Is the raucous song of life
Sung by the coq—and the Coquelicots.

When Aštart Sings

On *Astarte Syriaca*, by Dante Gabriel Rossetti

A star drops by, where she is consecrated—in Tyre,
Where the ever-vigilant tales of honor
inscribe the history of a land of epics.
For them, from them, she returns, emerging,
like a Phoenix nostalgic for life,
rising with the crimson coquelicots—
which, like Adonis, kiss life in every drop of death.

As she arises, they wait for the ariose vision.
There is a divine, diffused, profuse scent of glory
hovering above the crowds of the human Sea,
upon the stretched fingers of longing voices
reaching out to her, in breathless unison,
among the tremoring waves of a thundering
ground.

When Aštart sings,
She cries—and beams, facing Dido,
Striking heart, chord, and harpsicord,
as the moon finds its reflection in the radiance of
her smile.
The serenity of her soulful face and resonating
essence,
reach out to all in euphony like the first golden
threads of dawn.
And she sings…

As a tender breeze whistles out of her woodwind
being
blowing flute-breath along the vibes of an ancient
lyre
and the melody of the grandest lute.
She sings...
With conversing eyes and a sighted voice,
endowing all
With a fortune of tune, for tunes
Are the pulse of an indelible vision she dreams into
life.
She sings...
For glory, for love, for hope, for victory...
As her grand, free soul unleashes in a spinning
gust,
Engulfing all in her presence,
Moving the gentle leaves of being into harmonious
dance,
Whirling, wheeling, softly, swiftly, to the allegro of
the hurricane.
And she sings...

Shoe and Tell

On Barbara Graff's painting, *Cinderella Doesn't Live Here Anymore*

Under the illuminating eye of the Cyclops sky,
is a spotlight revealing a scene from a story
untold—a sequel:
She parks her shoes at the bottom of a once-barren
beanstalk,
now heavy with pareidolic budding branches,
spiraling up and down, like a descending dragon
and a scurrying squirrel.
The slippers, satin and not-glass, are now soft and
unbreakable,
retired vehicles of a tired maid.
Each to her own, one faces the East, the other ogles
the moon.
No longer working to impress with a perfect fit,
No longer awaiting a foot-seeking prince
and no longer that small. Wear and tear expands
the stiffest leather,
and calluses the thinnest skin.

Drawers, Slips, and Slits

an ekphrastic poem based on Salvador Dali's
Anthropomorphic Cabinet

"Keep them shut," they (or rather, *I*) say.
For it is best that mercury is kept at bay,
in a chest of buried treasures—of pleasures.
Winding down from crown to sacral bone,
sacred in double-helix mimesis, is a grander form
of pregnant drawers with little slips,
like a cascading waterfall, ending at the hips.
In them are tickets to Narnia, Neverland, and
Nevermind,
To fantasies of the future and abandoned pasts
behind.
In another is a muffled moan, a frozen bark in the
icy wilderness
of neglected dreams and haggardly hopes that still
press—
So, confess?

Lunar Rhapsody

On Pamela Chrabieh's painting collection,
Engaging Gazes

Amar, A Lunar Queen
Amar, to love
To breathe into the world of her eyes,
Wheeling, whirling, succumbing
to the music of the light--
Incantations of sin-aesthetics
In synaesthetic ecstasy.

I wonder what hides behind that silver face,
Beyond the crimson, grey, and gold.
What engaging brow, lash, or spinneret
In the orb-web of the gaze
Grazes at the hidden snake, slithering
through the notes of an inner orchestral gamut?

ii

Ludus

Or "A Thousand Poems"

By Roula-Maria Dib

You've written a thousand poems for me, my friend
--in your sapio-sudsy head…
in a world as real as this one,
where the ebb and flow of its soapy tides,
brush off and on that murky shore—
where all that can't but is,
all that shouldn't but will,
and all what's hidden is naked
under that ruthless, roofless hut:
your eyes.

A thousand thought-fruits you've yielded
and ignored the tree in vain—
rejecting, pushing, plucking,
peeling, carving, craving,
…and ultimately, feasting
upon the forbidden.

While gnomes gnaw the inner walls
of your cerebral cave, engraving them
with cuneiform fantasies,
a thousand lyrics you pen,
and sing to that tune of what I recognize
to be my own voice.

Salutations

A poem in the loving memory of my late grandfather

Salutations...
to the heart of a passed century, which continues to pulsate
with every fig, olive, and lemon tree.
Hats off to the hands and heart that once nurtured
The terra that you still give with your entire being, your all,
The new womb that gently caresses and carries
the memories of this life into the next.

And in every sweet, warm, winter brew is a psalm:
"Cleanse me with hyssop, and I will be clean."

Bouquets of damask roses, jasmines, and gardenias
shall crown those years of time and toil
with the scent and color of your dear soul,
commemorating the hopes, dreams, sorrows, and joys
that wrought those days of survival and adventure,
Circled by the compass of the great architect
you have loved
and served
faithfully.

Lavenders

With the night hushing irises away, lavenders call at
the break of dawn,
waving purple corollas at the vigilant apertures.
From a provincial path, and beyond the hinterland
of memory,
the healing embrace of a once-stranger dwelling in
my heart
thaws the ice-patched knees of my soul.
Defrosted, touched by frankincensuality,
I wonder at the sight of embosoming blossoms
in aesthesis, inhaling the sweetness of the vision.
For a moment, I am alive, awake, and here,
in synchronicity with an eternal dawn.
This moment is now, tomorrow, and forever.

It is you again, visiting. As ever, knocking at my
dream-doors,
gently caressing faith with lavandula petals.
This visit I shall return, willingly though
unknowingly
when amethyst bushes lead the way once again.
Miraculously, like a butterfly to a tea-rose,
I find myself on that much-trodden path
through the heart of an ever-open door.
And I kneel, drunk with love, lavender, and light.

Hold my Hand

"Mommy, if you hold my hand before I sleep, will we be in the same dream?"

You ask me whether, if I hold your hand while you sleep,
we can be in the same dream together—
and there's nothing I would want more.
So hand it over while it's tiny enough to wrap
entirely, within the world of my heart-sized palm,
protecting you, steering your way into life,
as you fasten me into the present, the gift
of the moment I never want to leave.
Life is here, now, this, and forever...
While you sleep, dreaming of rainbows,
your hand is the portal to the real world of color.

I cherish the petal-softness of your fingers,
which I saw bloom chubbily with time (and milk),
before slimming down into slender grips,
hardened only by blissful blisters and calluses—
side effects of joyful play on the monkey bar,
which, as you will learn, is a miniature of life.
I have oftentimes pressed my lips deeply
into the sweet, pillow-comfort of your hand,
and saw it embossed with my own kiss-prints—
bright and velvety, lipstick matching
your strawberries-and-cream scented

fluffy world of unicorns
that I hope you'll keep visiting, Forever.

I wonder, for how much longer do I get to clasp it
like this,
before your grip loosens in pursuit of adventure?
For this, hold my hand well now, until the embrace,
with all its tenderness, and talismanic touch,
becomes the eternal imprint that you always find
guarding the gates of the unicorn world you've built.
United forever, we can never be too far.

Nigredo

From a spout among the ebony waves,
I shake off a pair of tiny wings.
A flutter fans its way out,
Glossing away from the raven-dark depths, floating
off,
away from the confused mass,
toward the glowing embers of a mysterious flicker
…Like a moth to a flame I do not understand.

The Window of Life

A seed, a spark, a million grains—
You are Infinity in a Vessel,
well-cocooned.
You now glide among the galaxies
from one world into the other.
Push, charge
an exodus through the stars, a cyclone of ages
Whirling out from the ether, and in--to the earth.
Materialize, mortalize,
Maternalize.
Banging, breaking, breathing
at the portal where the beginning meets the end,
at the window where the serpent bites its own tail.
From water to air, a Word is made flesh,
Now heard, as life's trombone
Plays along your heartbeat, to the tune of your own
breath--the vent
At the ventana.

Aurora

So here we are again
In the now, in the know
A voice among the echoes
A flicker, a dance among the gleam
Ever an Indigo vibrancy— the iris of the mind
Encircling, vibrating rhythmically
In a cerebral dance.
Light of Light, very God of very God
Not unbeknownst to me, from the beginning
Another life, another realm
So far, yet so near
There, as it is here,
and nowhere.
Now as it was then,
Lights palpate, by vision
Whispering, waving
Calling from the tower--tor
A shout…thunder—Thor.
Baptisia blends
With the coat of many colors--
Pulling me closer, drifting forward
All the way to the golden thread
Pulsating backwards—special coding
To join the heart of Abraham,
Beating breath, throbbing light, flaring spirit,
Throwing crimson fuel onto the famished light.
'Thoughts stir. Inspiration stalks us,' she says.

Telepathy of healers, hearers
of secrets, seeing her Signatures in all things we
read,
forever contemplating, coming back
to listen, to love, to live.
And so we are here again, one more time,
And time again,
Knowing the truth,
Being us,
Being them,
Simply being,'
Many times, and forever.

A Poet in Love

Sometimes, this squid longs to be embraced,
pressed, and squeezed
until the flow of ink, as dark as sleepless nights, fills
a few hungry pages
with the gusto of this exotic delicacy.

At first, manufactured in its own body, along the
cardiac rhythm
of iambic pentameter,
is a confused mass. An *inkenstink* of the Wake...

But well-brewed, when it's love, ink and alchemy
carouse,
rising from squid to sacred.

iii

The Godmother

Mother, I have come home—weary and arid
I melt into your lap, and weep on the bolster
adorned with imprints of both my heart and soul.

My feet hurt from walking upon untrodden paths
to see the roses, and yet to be pricked by the thorns.
But Mama, he's tearing through, and he's almost
arrived.

She is in the attic, along with the whole kingdom,
waiting
to witness the awakening of the bride: not dead, but
long asleep.
The fruit of the vine hasn't raisined, but fermented
into wine.

Thank you for the wine, Mama. The real miracle
was unleashed with the liberation of my soul.
You've shown me how *in vino veritas*.

I feel your palms slowly cup mine, and pull.
In a moment of wine, I am bathing in the hyssop
water

Being washed
Being drowned
Being rescued

Simply being…

I see an olive branch nearby, amidst this oceanic experience.
Clytie emerges from the sea—only to root in the bosom of her new home.
Looking at and loving becomes looking like the light.

The Prodigal Daughter

So she got up and went to her mother...

The road back is always sweeter,
Like that fig she'll pick right after dawn, with that
ruby-red, metamorphic heart,
as striated as a scarlet rock formed by heat,
pressure, and wind.

The winding path leading home is a journey worth
every stumble and choking step,
like that hike up a rocky mountain, to a monastery
watchfully smiling at the return.
Or that march among the lavenders toward a holy
sepulchre
Or that digging of feet, knee-high with snow, eager
to stand tall with the cedars.

This road of toil and trial is but a means to the gates
of life.
She wears a lace of cyclamen flowers around her neck--
They say it shortens labor.

There is a sharp longing that awakens, startlingly,
like the prick of a thorn that heralds the rosebushes
nearby,
Or the buzz of a bee announcing a hidden kingdom
inside the spiny broom shrubs,

Or the sprouting slime signaling life within a snail's
shell.

Home is what it is. It's who I am, and where I am
lost and found
under the humbly lowering azure sky, crowning
mountaintops
with clouds and visions.
It cocoons in caves of pregnant darkness, where
lives are conceived
within rocks that sculpture every faith and thought-
form.

It's that gentle breeze in which daisies dance along
with dreams.
It's the outer face of the inner soul,
and the face behind the reflection in the mirror.

But while she was still a long way off, her mother
saw her and was filled with compassion for her; she
ran to her daughter, threw her arms around her and
kissed her.

Heraclitus Today

When your heel sinks into a stream once,
water keeps flowing, gently tapping onto a dimpling
present.
With memories in the making, carpets of film roll
and unroll,
Blinking stories, shedding incomplete scenes of a
half-baked crescent.

When you cannot step into the same river twice,
test new waters—catch another vessel.
Since the roots here were not deep enough to raise
this tree,
the soil turns, eroding images and an oft-sung
carol.

When nothing happens until something is moved,
Even the most deeply carved smiles become
fluxes--
Flowing against marble stagnation. Nothing stays…
but all dwells in the heart, before drifting into new
cups.

Iconic Existence

Keep her locked in an eternal smile, that loving
gaze
you see in your mind's mined cave deep within
your Self,
or in the symbol on the solid wooden surface.
Let her sing, but from her nether-world into yours.

Silence the singing icon to keep it alive,
never conjure the image or form it
in this foggy existence.

You kill the icon when playing Pygmalion.

Strength lies in the centuries-old wood, solid-tude
in solidity,
and purity in the hardness within its heart of gold.
There's reality in imagination and more life in
stillness,
One that is beyond the tangible and breathing.

Glossolelic, it speaks in echoes from the outback of
non-air.
When gods materialize, they die.
Only to be born again...

The Icon Speaks

Today she arises , beyond paint and gold…
A sweating, breathing image, not
of hard wood, but of solid being,
with a voice as soft as the vapor of her fading image,
as concrete as her emerging existence
encouraged into this world, where she speaks
melodies
as the other world—that of symbols—dissipates.
Clouds precipitate. And from that realm she moves,
serendipitously, into the world of synchronicities.
Whatever caused the conjuring, or beckoning?
There it was, the rapport between two realms,
Conversing, right before my eyes...
What have I called, pressed, or summoned
like an accidental portal into the sea floor, deep,
right into the lap of a cockle-shell,
Aphrodite blooms into this reality.

Insomnia

There is more to the scream
Than a Krakatoan sunset.
It munches on the dawning dream,
Of the bark-skinned gazette
Only to snatch away the lurking shadow,
Abruptly shocking life out of a small death.
Lest she cease to be, cease to know
Lest the hyenas of thought mock the fatty sheath,
Pulling, jerking away the suffocating ebony…
She collects the shards of logic—every scrape, every
scrimp,
Accosting this much-needed company
to outfox an existential imp.

The Maze of Consciousness

Like a dehydrating camel she walks around
the hall of mirrors, observing impressions of thirst
in every shard of glass
there, not here—
yet here, not there.
The world of reflections beams its aureate rays
insanely,
as the iris filters in what the cloudiness inside could
not fathom.
Perhaps a tremor could bring her back,
a sound, a touch, or any painstaking effort.
But a consciousness in nothing but name
lies in place of reality.
She looks at everything but sees nothing,
listens to all, but hears none.
The world is gone,
and perception is but a mere hovering
over the shadows.
She rocks over her own lap,
cradling nothing but the image of a dream.

The White-in-the-Waiting

Hope is a happy haunting, a sneaky, friendly ghost
colorless--alabaster at best.
That invisible wind behind the sails,
motor, mover, and fuel, might feel like a
fairy's kiss, a pinch of pixie dust,
or a genie hatching through a lamp's cervix.

The horizon blushes, bashfully
with the setting sun's pink promise of tomorrow
as Lover Sky winks at his enamored Earth,
whom he'll ogle again in the morning.

Hope is that thing... in every White-in-the-Waiting,
not in the light, but in the patient screen that awaits
it.
Hope is not a thing with colors, not a door, but a
pearly wall
propping itself for graffiti (of perhaps, a door?).

It is an ivory cast, coiled around a broken limb, waiting
for the chromatic cuneiform of loved ones' signatures.

It is still that thing with feathers, though:
a blanched, post-deluvian dove at the ark's door,
a message of rainbows forming,
an anticipation of color,
an invitation to life.

iv

Death of a Capitalist

In the beginning was the Word...
And while a sentence begins with a capital, never
does it end with one.
The first letter, towering arrogantly over its fellow
flowing phonemes
will be long-forgotten when a full stop anchors the
shore,
sentencing all characters to a period that lasts
forever,
when they fall like a deck of domino tiles, pips lost
among the rubble.
*For many who are first will be last, and the last will
be first.*

Reptiles and all brood of vipers do not perspire—
just like statues (of maybe equality, liberty, and
fraternity),
but leeches grow ungratefully on sweat and blood
until falling off the host
into a dreamless sleep.

Wordsearching

Eyes bob up and down,
      typewriter-left-and-right
before landing on the right tile
      in this visual hopscotch
on a hunt for some mysterious page sprites.
      Somehow, life is all a big game of words,
a hide-and-seek, a constant Search for the right term.
      Like homing pigeons, they teleport
thought-bundles, wish envelopes, and crystallizations
      Of unkempt feelings across ears and minds.
They knock on the door of the left frontal lobe
      And wait to be let in.
And suddenly, they wonder, like Goldilocks:
      Between the voice and the breath,
      The intention and the meaning,
      Which one is *just right*?
But what is that word for the word "word" again?
      that *mythos*, rendering us
      all gods in our own epics.
The jouissance continues. Found it.

A Trickster Triangle

Because we travel into the past at a fleeting split
second per millenia,
we see the people from two thousand yesteryears
again today.
A recurring trio onstage wears masks of strength,
cleanliness, and fidelity.

There was a man named Caesar, grand and august,
and we still give unto him what is his.
He wears the bay leaves of self-proclaimed
godliness.

The other man, Pilate, looks decent and clean.
We even saw him wash his hands. Got nothing on
that innocent lad,
or so he said. He wears a taintless shirt.

There was also a Judas, friend and follower.
Overambitious.
A good bargain of a chap—
worth thirty silver chunks. He seals with a kiss.

Here they remain, dancing the triangle, reappearing
in different places,
forms, and variations of purity—or lack thereof.
Never-gone tricksters, they wear bay leaves, clean
shirts, and kisses,

only to remove them, teaching us that not all that glitters is gold,

(it can be thirty silver pieces, for example).

Not everything washed is sterile,

and it only takes is one moldy embrace to rot the dozen.

Euripedes repeats: *often a noble face hides filthy ways*.

This was a story of long ago, yet way too young to be old,

for once upon a Caesar, always upon a Caesar.

We continue to sacrifice the lamb

and choose the thief.

Crucify him!

…and they blame it on the hordes.

…but never on the 'clean hands'.

To Savor and Relish

Whether it's lazy cake, banana bread, custard,
marble bundt, or a savory, salted log of fries,
when their airy little fairy-whiffs channel
my inner Peter Pan, they jump into
that black hole, where all is lost in translation
right beneath the shaded grove of the
cerebral cortex.
Into that storage room of scenes they pry,
rummaging through childhood memories, while
dallying with my emotional thermostat.

In retro-scrying, I see myself with friends and
siblings,
commencing the weekend around a Monopoly board
on a cozy Friday post-school afternoon, propped
on a carpet bedecked with an audience
of curious crumbs and candy-wraps.

I see my grandmother busy with life, filling up
cupfuls
of sweet cinnamon joy
as she hums love, an acoustic match
to the olfactory heaven she creates.

Some days we were scolded for staying out in the
rain—
Those were made of bittersweet chocolate.

There were mornings when we bit into an icy
winter day
 as our teeth guided the way through the warm
oregano pastry.
And those birthday parties, when cake was
everything
and life was one big vanilla puff and blowing out
the candles
was not an evil act of spreading germs.

We held brunches on the terrace, when the weather
allowed
a Sunday to live up to its name.

And those nights when grandma arrives, wrapped
up
in cloaks and shawls as she brings us a warm
thermos
of lentil soup, which, like her, remains temperate
despite the frigid world.

It's these images and aromas of winter that keep us
snug.
Despite the cold, we kept warm.

And today, when we're feeling gelid again,
we still reach out for these smells that lead those
walks down memory lane.
And defrost.

Chronus is a professional abductor.
But cake pays a handsome ransom.

Moonlighting

Sometimes I get fed up with the megalomania
of confinement, of being where I don't want
to be. But there's nothing that time or space can
do to limit the "vacate" in "vacations".
So I let the inner roar tame the outer lion.

The life-like whirlwind of boredom, only sets me
freer as I stare into the only source
of light, air, and noise I have: a small opening
in my awning window. I wish there was a Narnia
inside my closet—must be the lack of coats.

There was a full moon, a pink moon, and a ring of
fire;
I had exactly 5 cm to capture a glimpse
of my lunar company with my camera.
I squint, and then cover one of my eyes
for a sharper, clearer vision.

The glass is goosebumped, over-embellished
with polka-dots of acid rain, making
an awful see-through. With enough uncertainty
and unclarity in the world, I'd rather view
the Claire *de la lune* through that crack

no wider than my small hand. And I look.
And I see. And I marvel, overjoyed

at the concave droplet of silver in the vast,
ebony sky, dotting the i's of the world.
A wide aperture is in the eye of the beholder.

I could swear I saw it smiling several times,
And heard it whispering silent vespers of peace—
something to go with the friendly beam.
Per amica silentiae luna…

Sometimes, the only means of travel you have
is a train of thought. So I look at my desk
and commit metaphors of all types. A book
becomes another world, opening like
a street musician's accordion, with the

sweet tunes on a busy street…underailed,
I take my pen as a rail ticket and doodle
my destination on that tiny space
left on my groceries list. I glance out
another window, my laptop screen,

through which, while inhaling my coffee, I
finally see The Swinging City, greeting
me with softee vans, theatres, squares, books,
bookshops,
and galleries reverberating once more
with the heartbeat of a loving giant.

Let me shut my eyes
and just be there.

Scarce Resources

Gawking, unintentionally but professionally, like a rat among
busy city dwellers rushing to their affairs
in high heels and roller skates,
she listens, wondering why they are still choking on another platitude.
Regurgitated nonsense, acidic—burning with the attitudes
of offended barons, pedants, chefs, and two-year-olds—
repeats itself on another batch of speech bubbles,
like the ones you'd see between Magneto, Kingpin, and Loki
if they are to ever co-exist in the same comic strip.
Shrugging, she walks back into her cubicle, and imagines
that she is a kettle, carrying warm water,
with no tea bags around to flavor it while still hot.
She asks herself whether to pour out the tasteless drink
And doom it to eternal blandness is actually wise when you can
keep it in for other uses.
The reverie is cut at the squawking, honking sound of a beaky horn.
Noise pollution.
Another waste of precious resources.

Figs and Marrows

The words ascend, puffing upwards like heavy clouds.
A thick mist forms, heavy with lies,
tall with tales,
almost too high for earthen dwellers
who don't own a Jacob's ladder.
Verbs are tarred, floating high above the terra,
almost uppity towards *Tara*

Tarataratara

This cacophony along the scraping of the corer
is the song of an emptying marrow
and its hollowing out of substance.
A nightshade is what it is, shining with gator-like skin,
wearing a green garb, but hiding a void within

Falling into the basket, a marrow will never become a fig
and a mirror becomes an eyesore if lipstick's on a pig.

Immunity

Words unmask, as parentheses are lifted and
expressions spill,
                        untethered
out from a de-mummified mouth-in-verse, like
grains
of icing sugar, scurrying out of a tiny puncture in a
plastic bag,
                        no longer sweet.
Counting. People. Cases. Perhaps, cattle-like, in
herds. *Numbers*.
Out of breath, in many ways, suffocating on
forbidden air
                        and dreams.
What are lowercases in a world of capitals? Listen,
lulling
                        thoughts and questions
which shall remain unanswered, until further
notice, while we
                        sit back
and witness mass contagion, with its metabolic side
effects
of digesting facts, absorbing prejudice, and
assimilating fear.

The truth is held hostage in a game of hide-and-
seek, tucked
                        in some layer among the rubble

until it unravels, yawning awake, stretching in stark
nakedness,
                              wondering
where we were before pausing that video, freezing
time.
And as nations starve and die, people
conjure the phoenix, living in mythopoesis,
preparing, watching, waiting, vigilantly
for a miracle within the fertile ashes.
Resistance builds antibodies to misapprehension
and immunity to inscrutability of viral
news, tweets, and other toxic narratives that can be
altered
with the swift inflection of
                              perception.

Grapes

Dropping down, like jaded tears of summer joy,
are the hanging chandeliers of Bacchus,
dancing in the shade of the vine-leaf tent,
roofing, shading, and sketching silhouettes of
lovers, jesters, homemakers and merrymakers.
Not-mistletoe, but invoking and witnessing
countless summer kisses, sacrosanct,
and guarded by vine, verse, and litany,
the grapes, shoots, and arrows fulfill their mission.
In a *pas-de-deux* of the well-paired hosts,
Bacchus revels, patting the pirouetting shoulder of
Cupid.

It is the season when Dionysus is re-membered, at
every table
in woven straw baskets and plates—silver and
terracotta,
and in half-filled glasses
Of raki, pearl-white, aniseeded dreams,
Or rosé, blushing with damask-rose bubble cheeks,
Or sparkling gold of pinot alchemy
or the red passions poured from
those adamantine alabaster jars,
hosting the wedding at Cana,
toasting the boundless, lustrous tresses of the night,
which continue to glimmer at dawn.

Matinee

The silence of the sun
is broken by the whispers of the wind,
spooling among sinuous branches.
Sound…
Embossed with the cricket's early greeting,
is a tribute to Phoebus.
Voice…
The birds chime in, chirping at his chariot.
Meaning…
And there it was, from the very beginning—
the breath,
for ears to hear, skin to feel, and soul to sense
its heartbeat, rock-forming
of seven hues, seven tones,
and one dance.
Windsurfing, far away until trapped
in ink-incarceration,
is a womb-tower of immortal bliss,
which forms into being,
reverberating, un-searching.
It is a host, a lover, and a warrior
of truth.
Let's start.
In the beginning was the Word.

Twenty

With all that doublespeak, you'd think someone just stepped
into an Orwellian *Nineteen Eighty Four*,
but ended up crossing the bridge,
regressing to a *Nineteen Hundred and Nineteen*,
where old and new are in torsion, gyrating in and out,
in a *pas de deux*.
But the futuristic return to Twenty
is a jet lagging oxymoron
that can feel like the *Second Coming*,
as "Things fall apart. The center cannot hold".

One hundred and one light years later, dreams have lost elasticity,
making the most modest of them look daring.
Yet we can still arise and go now, for the *Inn is free*.
In it,
we can weave visions of a new normal,
and cook remedies for ramifications.
Destruction demands dawning, as night is to day
(and other analogies).

There is an image of Plato's man, round on all sides
with the heap of parables and poetics,
and furiously whirling cyclonic vortices,
like dervishes,

spinning to the rapid, staccato drumbeats.
But isn't this how we wash our clothes,
stir in the honey,
and run around the mulberry bush
so early in the morning?

And so the sun rises.

Lemonade

And so it happens that one day,
you may find yourself juggling
a few too many lemons.

But not in the way a street performer would do
in your favorite square, under the shredded clouds
and the bird droppings you always manage to
dodge.

When life gives you lemons,
usually, there's a citrine in the citrus.
Make them precious,
like gemstones in your palms.

To homeostasize the surrounding tartness,
and alkalinize the acidic
you find that perhaps,
it's best to slice them:
cutting out, cutting through,
you find yourself squeezing, pressing,
and sieving out the pulp.
Good stuff.

You sweeten without sugarcoating
and let the crystals merge
in a tintinnabulating stir.

Perhaps there's no harm in some current
cocooning,
in becoming the genie in your own bottle,
until it's safe enough to twist your way out,
swiftly, and unscathed.

It would then be smart to make lemonade,
upgrade to limoncello,
and fill up the space in the empty vial.

Cin.

Afterword

Simply Being…in a Reality that we Create

What this poetry collection does is share and amplify images of all the things that had informed me as the person I am today and the things I connect with on a daily basis, beyond the quotidian and the mundane: Love, myth, and art—in short, this collection is a celebration of all the things that make me, as well as humans in general, tick. These poems are expressions, or rather, live performances of archetypal realities; these are the things that are made alive through us, by simply being, which activates and encourages the spirit of art, myth, and love into existence.

The book is divided into four sections, each of which limns a different dimension of existence, or as the title of the book suggests, of "simply being": Ekphrasis, love, mythos, and world. The poems in the first section are ekphrastic interpretations of some paintings that have touched me personally, oftentimes stirring a parallel, mythical realm. The second section, on love, is a collection of poems on the many aspects and types of love, mainly romantic, maternal, familial, and spiritual. The third part covers the different challenges and changes we may face in life. The fourth section, penned from the recent heart of the matter, is a set of reflections on the pandemic-stricken world, written while under lockdown. In this part of the collection, the poems explore the many truths that have become unmasked in an era of *wearing masks*. Much of the poems here are read and filtered through archetypal manifestations of the trickster.

Hearing terms such as "the new normal," "new world order," "post-pandemic world" all re-ignite spiritual images that have been with me since childhood, manifesting themselves every now and then, but never as profoundly as this period of time. My sense of spirituality has been formed over the ages by stories—from the bible, myths, and fairytales. Being brought up in the Greek Orthodox tradition, there is a huge biblical influence in my work, found in allusions made in many poems such as the allusion to (Old Testament) Joseph in "Aurora," Byzantine iconography in "Iconic Existence" and "The Icon Speaks," Jesus's crucifixion in "The Trickster Triangle," Psalm 51:7 in "The Godmother," Noah and the ark in "The White-in-the-Waiting" (which is also a personal rendition of Emily Dickinson's "Hope is the thing with Feathers"), and the parable of the prodigal son in "The Prodigal Daughter." The figures alluded to in these poems are archetypes that have always spoken to me and expressed themselves in my life. During times of crisis, uninvited, they pop up again only to be welcomed with open arms—while we are witnessing what seems like an unveiling of a new dawn.

Moreover, images from myths, that also pay tribute to an inherent sense of spirituality, emerge in "Coquelicots" (Adonis and Astarte), "Starry Night" (Egyptian goddess Nut), and "When Astarte Sings" (Astarte again, obviously). Allusions to fairytales also appear in poems such as "The Godmother" (Sleeping Beauty) and "The White-in-the-Waiting" (Aladdin's lamp).

As I always tell my students, to write a poem is to take the world around you and recreate it according to how you perceive it. Not only to write about it as such, but also to experience your being through possibilities, by taking the ordinary and rendering it extraordinary, "where poor utensils show/ like rare objects in a museum" (1: ll. 29-30), as Hilda Doolittle says in her *Trilogy*. This is what I found myself doing often enough during lockdown, in a tiny apartment with no balcony, and no fresh air except for the few inches of open space I get by pushing my non-sliding windows out. Living on the 14th floor of an urban tower 72 floors high, while looking down and out from the window, I felt that the world was far, far away—it was the kind of reality akin to the one Rapunzel may have experienced. I wanted to travel back home, which I couldn't do of course, but I found my magic carpet through the medium of poetry. I traveled to the past though the smell of food, which made me not only rekindle, but recreate precious moments, like in the poem "To Savor and Relish," where I found myself superimposing childhood memories onto the present, like holding a souvenir that I brought back from a faraway land. I wanted the magic carpet to take me outside the window, where my feet can feel the Earth under my feet and feel the sky above my head and be able to see and marvel at all the clouds, birds, sunrises, full moons, and eclipses that were there. I mention this in the poem "Moonlighting," where I also convey my pining for travel, for being in London, strolling through the vibrant streets of the Swinging City. I was also homesick for my ancestral village in the Mediterranean, where I felt closest to all manifestations of my archetypal mother: Mother Earth as well as my biological mother, and all temples, shrines, and paths of the divine mother (Astarte, the Virgin Mary, and Saints like Tekla, Marina, Barbara)—hence my poem, "The Prodigal Daughter." I found that the best path to tread upon was the one that formed me, the world of stories, art, and storage of unconditional love. I saw the world as going through *a second wave of modernism*, and in the process, I found myself "making it new"— thereby making it real, making the surrealism of the world not only tolerable, but *embraceable*.

I knew we had hit somewhat of a collective katabasis as a human race, who was scared and terrified at the present and future; I felt that there had been too much narration was going on in the news and social media, which I found to be useless and oftentimes, spiking more anger and frustration among people, who were not only anxious and bitter, but more confused than ever. As if the pandemic was not enough, news about riots, wars, death, famines, and various forms of conflict were all what was highlighted. Indeed, these were dark times—dark with uncertainty, which, ironically, was the only certainty around. I felt the need to respond to, rather than narrate, what was going on around me—the need to look at the fecundity of a "pregnant" darkness, to flush out the benevolent part of the current state of the world, without denying the malevolent part. It was a time to make use of the indoors as a gateway to the "inner," the world of spirit and creativity. Every new life is preceded by the darkness of the womb. So I crawled into that womb, focusing on the goodness of love, and cocooning inside the world of archetypes through poetry, the language of the ineffable. During this time of heavy literalism, the world can use a bit more metaphor, more imagination, more Eros and connection with our inner creativity.

These poems, therefore, are an expression of and a response to the blessings in my life, the memories that I cherish, and all the great forthcoming changes and renewals that I look forward to. Every verse is a celebration of all the different aspects of existence that we can experience and reflect on. These are the many faces of life, of simply being.

www.ingramcontent.com/pod-product-compliance
Lightning Source LLC
Chambersburg PA
CBHW030028290326
41934CB00005B/538